by

**Torkom Saraydarian**

Published by

Aquarian Educational Group
P.O. Box 267
Sedona, Arizona 86336

Artwork by Joann L. Alesch

Printed in the
United States of America

Typography by
R S Typographics

Printed by
Banta West Inc.

Dedicated to
the
Fiery Servants of
Shamballa
Nicholas and Helena Roerich

## ABOUT THE AUTHOR

T. Saraydarian was born in Asia Minor. Since his childhood he tried to understand the mystery called man.

He visited monasteries, ancient temples and mystery schools in order to find the answer to his burning questions.

He lived with sufis, dervishes, Christian mystics and with teachers of occult lore. It took long years of discipline and sacrifice to absorb the Ancient Wisdom from its true sources. Meditation became a part of his daily life, and service a natural expression of his soul.

He has lectured in many cities; he has written numerous articles in occult, philosophical and religious publications.

He is a violinist, a teacher, a lecturer, a mechanical engineer, meteorologist, writer and philosopher.

*Shamballa* is an epic poem about one of the most beautiful legends in the world.

## OTHER WORKS BY T. SARAYDARIAN:

The Inner Blooming
Love, Beauty and Joy
The Science of Becoming Oneself
The Fiery Carriage and Drugs
Cosmos in Man
Bhagavad Gita
    translated from the original Sanskrit
The Hidden Glory of the Inner Man
Christ the Avatar of Sacrificial Love
The Five Great Mantrams of the New Age
The Hierarchy and The Plan
The Science of Meditation

"Like a diamond
glows the light
on the Tower
of Shambhala
He is there—Rigden-Jyepo,
indefatigable, ever vigilant
in the cause of mankind.
His eyes never close.
And in his magic mirror
He sees all events of earth".

*Shambhala*

by

Nicholas Roerich

# Prelude

The Legend says
there was only Space,
the self-existent
Causeless Cause.
      From Space
      emanated
      a Sphere of Fire
      radiating
      seven great
      energy waves
      in centrifugal,
      in centripetal
      constant motion—
      This was the breathing
      of the Fire.
      This was the emergence
      of a *fragment* from Space
      and coming into
      manifestation.
In the beginning,
—if there was at all
a beginning—
the rays of this Central Fire,
went every direction
into fathomless
pure Space,
and gradually
the points of these rays
hardened,

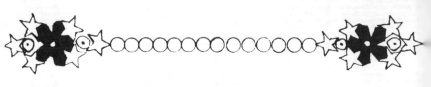

condensed,
materialized
and became atoms
in the space,
hung from the strings
of the rays.
An atom
is a dance of rays,
in which the rays
try to lock
to imprison
a spark of the
living Fire
and bring it
into denser
manifestation
by building walls
around it
from their
very essence.
       Atoms thus
       came together
       by the urge
       of the rays
       and reflected
       configurations
       existent
       in the heart
       of the pure
       Central Fire.
In the atom
in all atoms
a ray of the Central Fire
has
its anchorage.
Every atom

has a spark of the
Fire
as its center.
      Every atom
      has an urge
      to be a Sun.
Our Sun,
was an atom—
Our Sun
with its Solar System
is an atom
within
billions and billions
of Sun-atoms.
      Legend says—
      in each atom
      on all levels,
      there is the urge
      to go forward
      towards the Source.
This is the urge
to be.
This is the urge to create.
This is the urge
to contact, to be aware.
      This divine Fire
      rhythmically
      breathes.
      As it breathes
      it sends energy, wisdom,
      through its Rays,
      to the atoms
      and charges them.
         The atom,
         the point of a ray
         in the matter,

eventually
feels
inadequate to hold the charge,
and the atom disintegrates,
and the ray
builds a new vehicle
closer to the Central Fire...
This new vehicle can be
in the same plane
but a little more
unfolded
to be able to express
the voltage
of the advancing ray,
the advancing Spark.
As the charging
of the Central
Fire cyclically
continues,
the Spark receives greater,
greater stimulation
and one day
creates a totally different
kingdom
of its own—
the vegetable kingdom
comes into being.
Many millions of years
the Ray,
which appears as a Spark,
experiences more and more,
and
enjoys creating
more beautiful flowers,
bushes, trees in all climates.
The contact of the

10

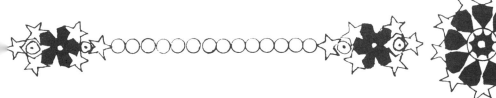

Spark
with the substance, closer to the Central Fire
creates
sensation in the atom,
creates fragrance,
creates colors
of thousand hues.
        The Spark enjoys
        mixing color, sensation, and
        fragrance . . .
        and covers the fields of Space
        with colorful beauty.
Millions of years pass.
Some sparks feel
that
this kingdom also
is a limitation
for their expansion.
They feel trapped
in the beauty of the kingdom
of vegetables,
and they try to strive harder
to break through and form
a new mechanism of contact
and expression.
        Some of them build
        the most elemental
        forms of the
        animal kingdom
        and
        during
        millions of years of experience
        and inspiration
        from the Central Fire,
        some Sparks develop
        higher forms

11

until they dress in the form
of an eagle,
of a horse,
of an elephant—
    Thus the animal kingdom,
    with all its variety
    comes into being.
But the Spark,
due to its own
experience,
through the joy and bliss,
through cyclic
inspiration
from the Central Fire
    awakens a little more
    and withdraws closer to the Fire.
    Some of the
    Sparks
    pass to another dimension
    and they form
    the next kingdom,
    the human.
        What a great victory
        for the Spark
        to be able to break the lure
        of lower kingdoms
        and face
        the responsibility
        to be human.
In the human kingdom
he develops
more
sensitivity,
emotions,
and he can
detach

cause and effect,
and use
a more refined
substance,
the mental.
    As he receives greater charge
    from the Central Fire,
    he tries harder,
    harder and harder
    to perfect his instrument
    of manifestation;
    his body,
    his emotions,
    his mind...
All these kingdoms
were not earthly
material
as we humans
understand the matter
but they were electrical, spiritual
phenomena.
    The rays travelling back
    into the Source
    built various kingdoms,
    as they proceeded
    on their way.
    Some of them even
    created
    planets
    as their bodies.
    Some of them even
    became Suns,
    in greater and greater
    magnitude.
    Those who travelled
    in affinity

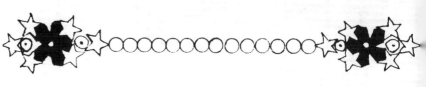

formed systems and galaxies.
Scientists
philosophers
will be surprised
if they read
what legend says
about man,
the stars
and the universe.

       The legend says
       it was the man
       that existed
       before the Sun,
       before the moon,
       before the earth.
It was the man
who came into
full blooming
before the earth
came into being.

       The earth,
       as it is
       is the body of a man
       who, billions and billions
       of years,
       unfolded
       in such a degree
       that
       he created a huge body
       as a field of education
       for all those rays,
       tiny lives who were
       wandering in Space
       on the ladder of existence.
A moon
is a disintegrating carcass

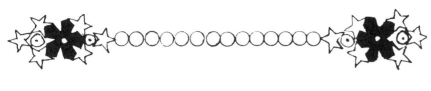

of a great, great life
who
once upon a time used it
as his vehicle.
Then left it, as we leave our bodies
when no longer we can use it.
       The legend says
       our planet
       is the body of that
       great Entity
       who died as the moon
       and was born
       as our planet.
The same Life
eventually
will manifest
as a Sun.
    This is our destiny
    and
    the destiny
    of all rays
    going back
    to Home,
    no matter
    what kinds of bodies
    they have.
       By the way—
       a Sun never cools down
       and becomes a planet or a moon.
       It melts away
       in the space
       and the Central Life
       proceeds on the path
       of its
       evolution.
The planets,

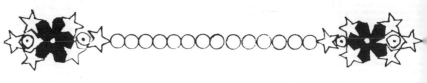

the solar systems,
the galaxies,
are schools for all
these rays
who are wandering
on their path
back to Home.

Many rays were attracted
to this planet.
Actually
the body of this
planetary life
is formed by the rays
on all levels—
atomic, vegetable,
animal, human,
Super-human,—
providing to all of these
education
and
discipline—
On some planets
man succeeded in surpassing
his level of achievement
and entered into
a higher kingdom, without an
intermediary,
          but legend says
          on our planet
          the Spark was stuck
          between half-animal
          and half-human
          level,
          and was not able
          to further

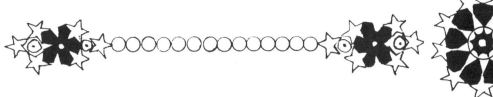

his evolution
because
certain failures
occurred on the moon.
But those who were
able to transcend that level
billions and billions years ago,
on various schemes of evolution,
and were watching
this planet
and the journey of the Rays, back to
Home,
came to help.
These were beings
who were called
Kumaras and
Solar Angels.
They taught man how to think,
how to talk,
how to build...
and those Sparks
who worked harder,
harder and harder
entered into
greater light, greater awakening,
and became
the teachers,
the kings,
the rulers
of the race...
Some of these great Ones
made a greater
breakthrough,
and they entered
into a new dimension
much closer to

the Central Fire
and
consequently
more charged,
more awake,
more enlightened,
more free.
    Some of these Sparks
    graduated from this kingdom,
    the human.
There is the Christ,
the Spearhead of evolving Rays
towards the Sun,
the fiery arrow flying
towards the source
of light,
of love,
of power...
    The legend says,
    the speed of the
    progress of Christ
    has no parallel
    in the history of our earthly
    humanity.
Then came other great
Ones, from other planets
Who were running the marathon
race
on our earth
as human beings.
Such as great, great Lord
Buddha,
Who,
the legend says,
was the last One
from Moon

18

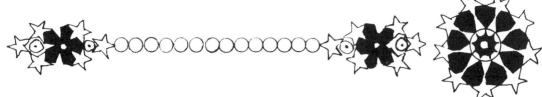

humanity,
Who continued His
race
on this planet
and eventually
achieved the Buddhahood.
Many other
great Ones
from our humanity or
from the different sources
continued
Their schooling
here on this planet
and eventually
graduated to higher
levels
on the path to Central Fire.
On our globe
all organized forms,
centers,
nations,
talents, geniuses, masters, angels, lives, souls
and monads
are the vehicles
of the Rays
traveling back to Sun.
When the Ray
builds
a physical body,
emotional
and mental bodies
and highly integrates these
by the forces of the nature
we call the ray
a personality.
When the ray

19

further
builds
higher vehicles,
and knows himself
being not his
vehicles,
we call him a Soul,
Who knows how to think,
how to love, how to will.
When the ray
further travels towards the Fire
and makes a contact
with the purpose of the Fire
we call him
an individuality...
a monad,
who is able
to master his vehicles
of expression,
who is able
to master time, space, energy, matter,
and
stand as a fountain
of compassion.
Here,
does not stop the evolution
of the Ray.
One day
he may be called
Heavenly Man,
if he builds a planet
as his body.
He may be called
a Great, Great
Heavenly Man,
a Solar Logos,

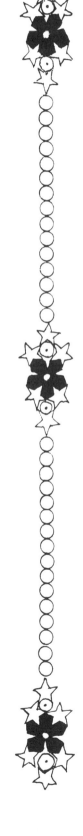

if He builds
a Solar System
and provides a field
of evolution
for billions of lives.
The legend says
there is no limit
to the
possibilities of
the Ray—
All manifestation
came into being
not because a god
created it "at the beginning,"
but because
the Rays from the Sun invisible
turned Their
faces homeward
and on Their journey
They created
form after form
to reveal
the mystery
within matter,
within the Ray; within the Central Fire.
Thus came all forms, all planets,
all suns,
all constellations,
all galaxies
and all, all
manifested phenomena.
This human form
was not
manufactured
by a god
in the garden

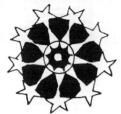

of Eden
in one day...
It was the Spark of the Ray
of the Central Fire
who in
millions and millions of years
of heavy labor
built the form
after the configurations
within the Central Fire.
    Still every spark of life
    is occupied
    in building new bodies,
    new vehicles
    on higher and higher planes.
        Forms are built
        as a
        mechanism of contact,
        to analyze and synthesize
        impressions,
        to be one
        with the whole
        but sustain
        individuality,
        to be one
        but apart.
    Only thus the Living One
        can know
        Himself
        as one in essence
        but
        manifold
        in expression.
    Thus,
    my friend,
    you and I and all others

are
a part of all that
exists,
of all that makes
things to exist.
No one is an island
or
an isolated,
separate
form
or being.
Your root is
in the Central Fire.
You are the Fire
in its true sense,
going back towards Thyself.
All these
millions of years
you did not
realize it,
but now you can
feel that
you are
a Ray, in the process of
withdrawal into the Central Fire.
Many, many millions
of forms
you created
in your desperate
search
for your Self—the Fire.
And now
at this stage you can
look back
on your journey
which started

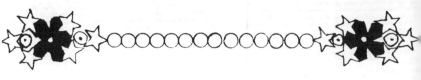

in the darkness of space
and
comes closer, and closer
to the Central Fire.
    My friend,
    there is a great
    joy
    in understanding
    the reality of your existence...
    not only
    yours
    but all, all, all
    existence.
All forms of life
in all kingdoms
are rays,
projected from the Central Fire,
the root is the Fire,
you are the Fire,
they are the Fire,
all are one
one,
One,
ONE.
      One Fire
      and the rays...
      This fact is the source
      of all love,
      of all understanding,
      goodwill, harmlessness,
      striving,
      compassion,
      brotherhood.
This fact,
my friend,
formed groups, formed nations,

United Nations,
and will form
One Humanity.
    Then humanity as a whole
    will step
    into
    a higher expression
    into a higher dimension
    closer to
    Central Fire
    beyond, beyond
    the manifestation.
        Humanity then will be
        The Hierarchy of the planet,
        The Shamballa
        of the planet
        and will move
        higher and higher.
Thus, my friend,
when the rays
from the planets
reach the Sun
with wisdom
and deeper experience
The Sun
as a whole
will make
a breakthrough
in its cosmic
evolution
towards the great
Central Fire
from which
It was emanated
as a ray,
and acted as an atom

once
upon a time,
and now going back
as a sphere
of will, of love and light.
Our Sun,
my friend,
is a station on the path
to the Central Fire.
Our Sun is a ray, is a life
going back
to the
Central Fire.
Our Sun, my friend,
is a door,
is a path
for all those rays in this system,
who are unfolding
and going back
Home.

On our planet
our Sun has
an eye
and that is the
SHAMBALLA.

# The Legend of Shamballa

From the seven mountains of fire,
from the seven oceans of color,
from the seven
forests of old,
came the legend
of Shamballa.
    The Gobi desert
    was a great ocean.
    In the midst of the ocean,
    there was an island.
    It was called
    the "White Island,"
    as all Those Who were living there
    had bodies
    formed by
    substance of light.
    The radiation of their bodies
    as a whole
    was filling the Island
    and the Island
    was shining as a huge
    diamond on the blue great ocean.
        It had a king
        spoken in all
        world legends.

He was called
The Youth of Eternal Springs,
The Ancient of Days,
Melchizedek,
The Mighty King of Righteousness
and peace,
Rigden Jyepo,
The Warrior,
The Initiator,
The link between Cosmos
and planet,
The Sanat Kumara.

This planet,
our earth,
is the body of the most
Ancient One.
A great Life
Who is
on the path
of His Cosmic evolution.
The Solar System as a whole
is the body
of a greater,
greater Life, traveling
on the path of
Infinity—
    Our planet
    in the body of the Solar System
    is a center,
    is an organ
    of the Solar great Lord.
By the ordinance
of the Solar Lord,
lives are going through a
unique evolution on this earth,
Lives sent here by the
great Karmic Laws
to learn,
to be purified,
to be unfolded,
lives from the moon,
from other planets,
from other Solar Systems,
from Space where

they were awaiting opportunity
to continue their evolution
in physical manifestation and
lives individualized
from the animal kingdom.
All these lives,
numbering 60,000 million,
are cyclically coming into
and going out of manifestation.
> There was great darkness,
> great inertia in the hearts of human
> beings.
> The earth was
> very slow in its time table
> of evolution.
The most Ancient One,
after consultations
with Great Lords, Manus and Moon Lords,
raised His Voice
and asked for help
from Cosmic great Lives.
> Far away in space
> the call was heard
> and one hundred and five
> fiery beings,
> headed by
> the Eternal Youth
> responded to the call of
> service,
> to the call of sacrifice.
> Leaving
> Their blissful abode
> They came to this
> earth of labor.
They descended
upon the Island,

The Island of beauty,
silence, serenity and purity.
    For the first time
    in the history
    of this planet
a group of shining Ones,
sat for a meeting
to discuss
the evolution of humanity
and the transfiguration
of the planet
as a whole.
    The presiding One
    was
    the most Ancient One, who
chose
the Eternal Youth,
Sanat Kumara,
as the head
of the Most Holy
Assembly. . . . .
    They sat
    within a fiery rainbow
    all dressed
    white
    and with seven stars
    on Their heads
    They contemplated
    and discussed for nine years
    about
    the Will of the Solar Lord.
    They analyzed The Will
    and formulated it
    into twelve Laws.
    The law of synthesis,
    the law of attraction,

the law of repulsion,
the law of economy,
the law of cycles,
the law of vibration,
the law of cohesion,
the law of disintegration,
the law of magnetic control,
the law of fixation,
the law of love,
the law of sacrifice,
and other laws
subsidiary
to the major laws.
The legend says
dividing these laws
into seven Groups
They formed the foundation
of the seven
major
Ashrams,
Where the Great Ones discussed
the possibilities
to utilise
these laws
for the upliftment
of all kingdoms,
for
the awakening
of the human soul
as an individual,
as a group,
as a nation,
and then
as one Humanity.
The result of this solemn study
was the PLAN

for this Planet.
Thus the Will of the Solar Lord
was translated
into the Purpose
and purpose
into
the Plan.
The legend says:
throughout ages
the Great Ones
developed and adapted
the Plan to the needs
of the kingdoms
on the Planet.
And in due time
they built
great universities
and mystery temples
to educate humanity.
        The seven Rays
        pouring out of the seven
        mighty stars
        of the Great Bear,
        were the seven mighty rivers
        of inspiration
        of the Seven Ashrams.

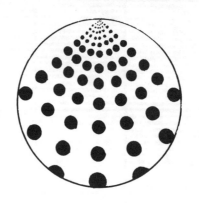

The Plan was divided
into seven
branches,
as the seven colors,
as the seven notes,
as the seven divine Rays.
        They named these branches
        politics,
        education,
        philosophy,
        arts,
        science,
        religion,
        economics and finance.
After the Plan was ready
They asked
from Cosmic sources
the help of millions
of fiery spirits
Who wanted to have experience,
to do experiments,
and serve.
        They were called by
        many names:
        Solar Angels,
        Fiery Meditators,
        The Sons of mind,
        the Watchers,
        the beautiful Ones,
        the flowers of love, of joy, of bliss.
They came and watched
the condition of the planet,

"It is too early to do
   something serious."
They said
and departed.
      The second wave of
      visitors came
      after many centuries
      to see if They could do
      something
      for humanity.
            They observed humanity
            and from Their
            essence
            They put a flame
            in the mental substance
            of the animal man.
            And for the first time
            man was able to use his mind,
            and to grow.
Ages passed,
and the third wave of Angels came.
And They saw
The flame
planted by
former angels.
"We can use
   that flame"
   they said,
"as a station,
   to help man,
   to watch him,
   to inspire him,
   and lead him
   into greater awakening,
   into greater realizations."
      Thus, they descended

35

and entered into
the electric sphere
of the human being.
The legend says
many thousands of men
were not able to hold
the charge of power,
generated by these angels,
and their brains
were burned out,
but those who could
handle the charge
had the first thrill
of using the mental
substance
and to think.
The Spirit, sleeping
within them,
had a great shock,
and the cycle
of
awakening began.
All Solar Angels
are the members
of the Hierarchy,
the Assembly of the Holy Ones.
Each Solar Angel
stands
as the representative
of the divine Plan
in man.
They are the embodiment
of the love
principle.
They are also the
executors

of the Karmic Lords
in man.
All our motives
are open to them,
They are watchful eyes,
no action,
no emotional reaction,
no thought
can be
hidden
from Them.
The Lords of Flame,
as They were called
tried to come in contact
with the Spark,
deep, buried
in man.
They used the method
of meditation,
inspiration
and impression.
Age after age,
They awakened
greater response,
greater aspiration,
striving
within man.
Those who worked hard,
those who served in spirit,
became
co-workers
of these angels
to further the
Plan
on all levels
of creation.

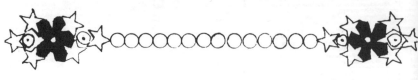

Accomplishing
such a
great progress
on behalf
of humanity,
The Stronghold,
Shamballa,
as a group of
hundred and five
took another
action.

    Some of Them
    vested
    Themselves in human form
    and
    created groups, races,
    nations,
    and became their
    divine Rulers.
    These great beings were the
    first
    Kings
    of humanity.
        They organized great labors,
        They created
        great tension
        between race and race,
        and humanity
        felt Their power
        and worshipped Them as gods.
There were
seven Heads,
and
seven branches
of human striving,
labor and toil.

They chose
special spots on the earth
where beneficient Cosmic Rays
were crisscrossing each other,
forming energy vortexes,
and on these spots,
They built
Their great
educational institutions
for the seven
branches
of
human learning.
Great symbolic dances
were used.
Colors and sound were used.
Heavy labor
and pain were used
to awaken further
the Spirit of the human beings.
The schools They formed
were not only
on the plane physical.
They had schools
on the plane astral,
schools on the plane
lower mental
so that the race
as a whole,
whether in body
or out of body,
had a chance
to proceed
on the path
of unfoldment.
        Schools were divided

39

into
three sections,
preparatory,
advanced,
and
schools of Initiation,
where the most sacred
rituals,
ceremonies
were enacted and demonstrated.

Thousands of years
passed,
and the human soul, the human ray,
began to bloom.
    Some men entered
    mystery schools
    and went through
    discipline,
    education,
    life after life
    until one out of every million
    became a disciple,
    who cooperated with the
    King,
    with the heads of the
    schools,
and thus
the pilgrims of light
holding each other's hand
travelled the way,
and became Initiates
of the lesser,
and
greater
mysteries.
    As the enlightened Ones
    increased,
    one by one, the fiery
    Kumaras
    left this planet,
    for higher realms
    of our galaxy

41

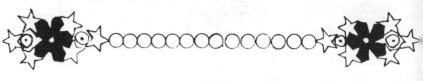

to continue Their fiery journey
in Infinity.
Only seven sacrificial Ones
remained with us.
Three of Them
serving as
the esoteric Kumaras,
as higher Centers
of three divine, unnamed
energies.
The other three
are related to Hierarchy,
to humanity,
and they change,
cyclically.
The Lord of the World,
Sanat Kumara,
remains with us.
He is the great Sacrifice,
the Silent Watcher,
the Initiator,
the King.

Our planet is an organ,
or a center,
in the great Solar System.
Six of our Kumaras,
are the links
between
six other planetary schemes
and our earth.
Seven Kumaras
are seven flames,
seven Spirits
before the throne,
the seven

head
centers
of the Ageless,
heavenly Man of our
planet.
The Hierarchy,
where the principle
of true love
developed to its highest,
was a center
formed
by Kumaras.
Now, at this point
of the human history,
men who reached
liberation
and
mastery
form the Center of planetary
education—
The Hierarchy.
This was a great
victory
for Kumaras and humanity.
Throughout ages,
all great Teachers
were direct
Rays,
coming out of the Hierarchy
to carry out
the message given to Them
by the Heart of the
Hierarchy.
All great religions are
faint echoes of Their
crystal clear voices

Who came to teach
the unity of life,
the healing power of love and beauty,
the value of labor
and striving,
the immortality of the spirit
and the path of Infinity.
All mystery schools in
the past were organized
by the direct disciples of
these Great Ones.
They were the Ones who taught
the science of rulership,
law and order.
This was the science of
harmony with the
purpose of the Lord
of Shamballa.
All great leaders
who are dedicated to
the human cause
are inspired from Him.
As His disciples increase
He will be the One
Who will rule humanity
as the only King
for eternities.
They were the Ones Who taught
the art of education,
the art of mastering
the vehicles of the soul,
and expanding the awareness
towards Cosmos.
They were the Ones Who taught
the love of wisdom,
the meaning of life,

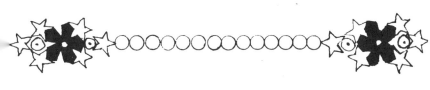

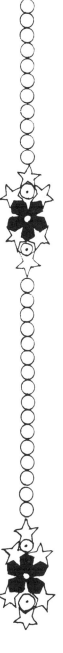

and matter,
and the relation between.
They taught the science of beauty,
The science of music,
the science of color,
the science of movements,
the science of the beauty in form.
This was the science
to awaken the sleeping
beauty
in each man.
They were the Ones Who taught
the concrete sciences;
how to make fire,
how to plant,
how to use the wheel,
the lever,
the water,
the earth,
the air.
All sciences
given to us,
are the pages
from the book of life—
The Secret Doctrine of Ageless
Wisdom in Shamballa.
Every true scientist
knows in his heart
that flashes of light
dawn
in his mind
when he
does all
that is possible for
human
beings,

and raises his mind
into peace
and waits.
Shamballa
sends fiery messages,
golden seeds
of wisdom and knowledge
to all those
who cultivate their minds
in true meditation
and
learn to penetrate
into the realm of Peace.

They were the Ones
Who taught
the art of worship,
the art of devotion,
the art of aspiration and
upliftment.
      Great temples were erected
      by the
      Master
      Architects.
            Those who built the pyramids,
            were the disciples of the
            Great Master Architects.
            That is why we can not
            yet solve
            the secrets of
            Their knowledge.
In great temples
They taught
the mysteries of life
in dramatic movements,
in colors and music.

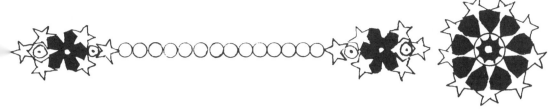

They taught
the great rituals
the science of ceremonial magic,
the economics, the labor
and management.
　　All these
　　They taught,
　　and when They saw that
　　Their disciples
　　could carry on
　　the process of enlightenment
　　They withdrew to
　　mountains
　　and jungles
　　and kept
　　watchful eyes
　　on the affairs of humanity.
Each of the seven departments
of human endeavor
is under the guidance
of a great Lord
Who acts
as a point of inspiration,
without
interfering with the free-will
of humanity.
Thus Hierarchy stands
as a source of Inspiration,
and
as a fiery wall of protection
for humanity.
The legend says
the Masters are more aware
of the affairs of the world
than any
human being on the earth.

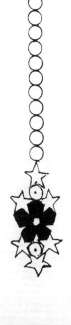

Many failures registered humanity,
many successes,
but in the darkness
of the history of the human race
a light always
was thrown
by the Brothers of humanity,
the Beacon of Shamballa
was always
guiding—
is always guiding
until the last ship
finds the way
to its lofty
destination.
   Shamballa, Shamballa,
   where the Cosmic Intention is
   known.
   Shamballa, Shamballa,
   the Magnet
   of light, the Magnet of love,
   the Magnet of will, and power,
   the Magnet that pulls
      all atoms,
      all cells,
      all men,
      all nations
      toward the Future,
      toward great,
      and greater
      achievements, and
      mastery.
   Shamballa!
   Shamballa!
   the Father's Home,
   where will return
   every prodigal son.

Tell me, O wise one,
where is now Shamballa?
"Shamballa, the Tower,
is in the space,
built by subtle etheric substance.
Shamballa
is on the earth too
in a hidden sacred valley.
Shamballa
in the space
is a diamond
raised from great ocean
to the space.
It stands as a
pyramid
formed by streams of fiery
energies.
All its mansions
are built by the substance
of light.
It is beyond the clouds,
but in direct contact
with all
its members, Initiates
and disciples
living in any plane
and
on
any
place of the earth."
   There He, the Kumara,
   as a Diamond Soul

49

never closes His eyes,
He traces each flame
of spirit
coming out of darkness
into the light.
He senses the labor
and striving
of His beloved ones
who age after age
try to master
time, space, matter,
death.
He registers the names of all
those,
who are working
for righteousness,
for peace,
for beauty,
for purity,
for light,
  and in rare moments
  He sends His joy,
  in a beam of
  light,
  into their hearts.
All humanity,
even
all living forms,
are considered His
children.
He cares for each
flame of life,
to lead them
age after age
to the path,
Home.

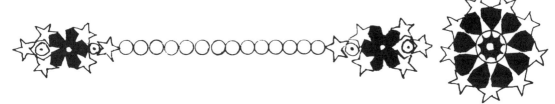

All races of all colors,
all tribes,
all religions,
all faiths,
all beliefs,
all knowledge
        are for Him
        different gardens
        where His children
        learn
        and
        mature.

"Below
    the heavenly Center,
    On earth there is also
    The Shamballa,
    where
    initiates and great disciples
    are invited to go and rest
    and be charged
    and once more to return
    to the field
    of greater, heavier labor.
    No one can
    enter the gates of
    Shamballa
    unless he receives
    the call of Shamballa.
    Shamballa
    is paradise
    on the earth,
    Trees, flowers of rare beauty,
    The music of aromas,
    the music of colors
    The symphony of waterfalls,

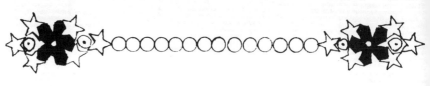

the unmovable
serenity.
    Electric walls of many miles
    protect
    the gates of Shamballa,
    fiery storms
    surround the
    subterranean
    passages to Shamballa.
Many servers of the human race
visited there,
when they gave Their utmost
to humanity,
and heard the sacred call
"Kalagiya"
Come to Shamballa.
At this time
there are many
who
are on the road
to Shamballa.
    Those who strive
    for unity of mankind,
    Those who do not
    exploit
    other beings, but serve and sacrifice,
    Those who adore
    each flame
    in every heart,
    Those who do not
    any more have the
    interest to possess,
    to enslave,
    Those who are not
    anymore
    burdened by the vanity

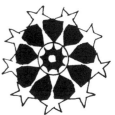

of their race, nation
and religion,
but are open to the values
of mankind,
to the interests of one humanity
They are on the road
To Shamballa—

Can any man
approach
the great heavenly Center of power,
the Stronghold, O Wise One?
"It is possible,
when you make
a contact

with your
innermost essence,
then the Master in your heart,
who is watching
your evolution
throughout ages,
    gives you a
    chance
    to visit
    the outer court of
    Shamballa
where you can see
the etheric statue
of Christ,
as the first human being,
Who,
in His marathon race of
evolution,
reached the Father's
Home, the Stronghold,
and heard
the voice
of the Eternal Youth—
    "My beloved Son
    the Resurrected One."
Thus through His
achievement
Christ became
the Way
between humanity and
the Father's
Home.
OM. OM. OM.
Glory to Him.
    He is called in the East
    by

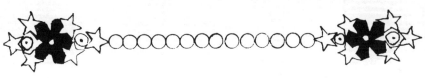

various names.
He is the Kalki Avatar
the Bodhisattva,
the Maitreya,
Imam Mahti,
The priest forever after the order
of Melchizedek,
The Christ,
the Desire of all nations.''

Shamballa
has four gates
and three doors.
	The first gate
	is *loneliness,*
	the second one *detachment,*
	the third one
	*isolated unity,*
	the fourth one—*purification.*
These are the four ways
which stretch
before the disciple of the Lord
of the World.
They must all be trodden
before the inner being
is released,
and the liberated Sons of God
can enter, at will
the four gates."
	*Loneliness Gate the First*
	is the withdrawal
	of the human soul
	from physical,
	emotional
	and mental
	interests.
	It is an intense
	inner focus
	when nothing else
	exists for you
	except
	the vision of divine Home,

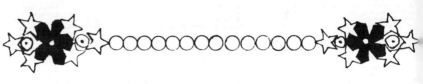

the summit
of human
striving.
    Step by step
    you climb
    the path of silence...
    the path on which
    you only
    must
    depend
    on what you are...
*Detachment is Gate*
*the Second*
when no longer
anybody,
anything
delays your feet
on the path.
One by one
you leave behind
the toys
of your
childhood,
sometimes even with a pearl
of tear,
but you continue to
climb
in greater, greater, greater
joy!
This is the path of freedom.
When you
sense
and realize
that you can do
without the chains
of many forms...

58

you stand in the
sphere of your light, love and power,
Without creating any response
from the objects,
from the levels,
from the ties,
of the past.
In a detached
state of soul
you still love people,
but you do not let
the inertia,
the glamours,
and illusions,
of their
personality
touch the Lotus of your being.
This leads you
closer to gate the third,
*Isolated unity*
You are one,
but
isolated,
as the leaves of the lotus
on the water of the
lake.
You are one with the essence,
but have
nothing to do
with the sheaths of human beings.
You hear,
you know—
but,
you
are
silent.

59

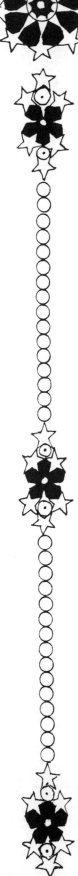

No thrill from the world
below
can evoke
any response
from you.
You live on the plane
of
the liberated sons of
Shamballa
and assimilate and radiate bliss,
joy and light,
compassion
in all
directions to all beings.
"You are in the world
and yet not of the world."
Isolated unity
brings you to the gate the fourth,
*purity.*
"Blessed are those
who are pure in heart
for they shall see
God."
On this path not only our
vehicles of manifestation
but also
all our motives are purified
and our heart
is a temple of the
Most High.
Only through such a purity
can the
warrior of light
penetrate
into the gates of Shamballa.
Four gates,

60

the foundation—the Shamballa
upon which
the Holy pyramid
of Shamballa towers
into the ethers—
shining as a mighty
Diamond
with three ruby doors.

Three doors of
Shamballa
leading the initiate
deeper
into the
Council Chamber of the Lord.
The first door
opens
into the first floor
towering by
many mansions of the "Father."
This door is called
*the door of Reason.*
Reason is the light of intuition,
straight knowledge,
by which man sees the things
as they are.
This door will be opened
to those
who throughout the ages
demonstrated
the faculty of seeing
the things
as they are.
Through age-long
experience
and labor
eventually
they will be able
to raise their focus of awareness
to such degree of power
that it will make

the man
able
to approach the door
and even
pass through.
    Extreme danger exists
    for the man
    who tries to enter
    this door
    with distorted mirror
    of his mind.
In the sphere of
Shamballa
no illusion can penetrate,
no distortion of truth.
When pure reason
is achieved
the traveler on the path
for the first time in his life
realizes
the meaning of Love.
He turns into
a stream of love divine,
and merges
into the ocean of compassion.
    The second door
    is
    *the door of will.*
    Will
    is the flame of the spirit,
    it persists,
    it endures,
    it strives,
    it masters.
All obstacles
help the fire of will

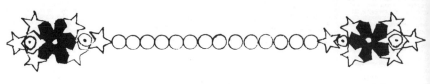

to grow.
Will reflects the purpose
of the great
Lord,
and once the reflected
images
get clear,
the will increases
tenfold.
As the will penetrates into
purpose,
man becomes a part
of the
divine Plan.
Every act of persistence
on the path of
the good,
on the path of Beauty,
on the path of Truth
shortens the path
between the man
and the door
of the will.
Every act of striving,
every act of self-mastery,
every act of sacrifice
builds
bridges on the path
to Shamballa.
Every act of endurance,
every act of patience,
makes you feel
the warmth of the heart
of the great One,
who watches your
steps on the

Path,
and you whisper
through your heart
"Not my will, but Thine be done."
　　The third door
　　of Shamballa
　　is the door of
　　*Monadic sense*
　　*of essential duality.*
　　　　a name, a symbol
　　　　of something very pure,
　　　　beyond our
　　　　comprehension.
　　But as humans we may say:
　　when you reach a stage
　　of unfoldment,
　　on which
　　for the first time
　　you can separate yourself
　　from the substance and see
　　substance as the not-self,
　　and see yourself
　　as the Self,
　　an individualized space
　　apart from
　　any vehicle, any form
　　in which you may be found at
　　that time,
　　you are closer to the
　　door the third
　　of Shamballa.
　　Three doors,
　　in front of which
　　fiery Angels
　　stand guard.
　　　　Three doors,

three spheres of electricity,
through which no one can pass
until one reaches
to the voltage of
the doors.
　　These three doors
　　are reflected
　　in our head;
　　the pineal, the pituitary
　　and the carotid glands
　　and then
　　corresponding centers
　　in the etheric
　　sphere.
When an initiate
passes through
these three doors,
we are told that,
　"He then faces
　　the life,
　　all events,
　　all predeterminations,
　　all wisdom,
　　all activity,
　　and all
　　that
　　the future
　　may hold
　　of service
　　and progress
　　from the angle
　　of the pure reason,
　　of true, spiritual will,
　　and of
　　highest possible
　　focused relation.

The mystery of relationship
becomes revealed to him.
Then the entire
scheme of evolution and
of the intention of the One
in Whom he lives, and moves
and has his being,
becomes clear to him;
he has no more to learn
within this planetary
scheme:

he has become
universal in his attitude
to all forms of life,
and is also
identified
with the
'isolated unity'
of Sanat Kumara.''

The Legend says
There are great great ones
In Shamballa.
They are called
"The supernal Three,
The Radiant Seven
The Lives embodying
forty nine fires—
The Buddhas of Activity,
certain
Eternal Spirits from Venus,
from Sirius, from
different Constellations,
and some Chohans
of first Ray—"
  All These are part
  of the Council Chamber
  of Shamballa.
All these members
are great
great
Initiates.
  An Initiate
  is a center
  of energy,
  is a fountain
  of energy,
  is a receiver
  of Solar
  and Cosmic impressions.
  Each Initiate
  is also a
  transmitter.

68

All members
of Stronghold
together
form a vortex
of stupendous energy.
    Energies coming
    from planetary,
    Solar
    and Cosmic sources
    pour into the great chalice
    of Shamballa.
These energies,
charged with
the fiery purpose of the Lord
of the World,
are the source of wisdom
and power
of the Hierarchy
and leading torch
for humanity.
These energies as a whole
are the
Energy of Shamballa—
which
    throughout ages,
    came in contact
    with humanity
    through the members of
    Hierarchy as a whole
    but, few times in history
    it bypassed
    the Hierarchy
    and poured down to humanity directly.
The legend says
it poured down first time upon humanity,
and created the right

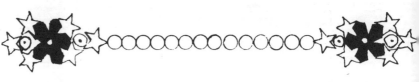

condition
for the implantation
of the principle of the mind
in the animal man.
This gave birth
to human soul,
awakening him from age-long
inertia
and sleep.
In Atlantean days,
when the forces of materialism
took control
over humanity,
Shamballa released
another stream of energy
and Atlantis, which was possessed by evil
forces, was submerged.
    The great leader
    at that time
    was informed
    to save the faithful.
        All that was in Atlantis,
        today
        is under the mud of
        the ocean.
Touches of the energy of Shamballa
were felt
1425,
1825,
1900,
bringing great advancement
in all departments of
human endeavor.
    "It awakened
    man's thinking
    in a new

and
comprehensive way,
produced
great
ideologies.
    It aroused
    their massed
    desire..."
    and also
    flamed the fires of destruction
    on the
    three planes of human
    endeavor.
The great war,
1914–1945,
was the reaction of humanity
to these forces.
    The energy of Shamballa
    is destructive
    when there are
    obstacles on the path
    of evolution.
        It is the human reaction
        or the response
        that makes the energy
        destructive
        or an agent
        of resurrection
        and release.
            It caused war,
            but also
            released the energy of the atom,
            formed
            the great
            United Nations,
            formulated

human rights,
four freedoms
and
the age of the
inner and outer
space,
an age of universality,
and global communication.
It poured down
again
1975.
We are told
a great destruction
started on the mental
plane.
All thoughtforms
of separativeness,
totalitarianism,
exploitation,
slavery,
are under the fiery hammer
of this energy.
As a burning fire,
it is cleaning
the polluted sphere of the
human mind,
and preparing
the age of
sanity, freedom, love, beauty.
This burning up
is leaving behind
the ashes, and the
trash,
which we can see
pouring out
through

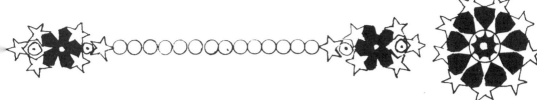

the current
mediumistic, spiritualistic,
movements and distorted politics.
Low psychism
in all its forms,
witchcraft,
hypnotism,
black magic,
communes dedicated
to sex
and vanity,
are the residue of
this great destruction
on the mental plane.
The pipes of the new age
energies
must be washed out
before we have
the clear water of
ageless wisdom—
the pearls of light
and beauty
from Shamballa.
Humanity registered a great
advance.
Because of the increasing
Sons of light
the third world war
was arrested,
in spite of
the endeavors of the
powers of darkness.
New bridges
are built
between great powers.
The vision of the one

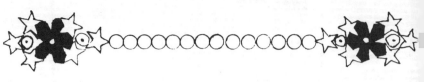

world,
one humanity
is so clear now in the
eyes of the youth,
even the blind in spirit
can sense it.
The power of the unity
will overcome
the forces of
disunity.
Man will feel more and more
as a citizen of
the world.
Man will love
all men,
nothing will come
between man and man,
not color,
not religion,
not sex,
not any ideology,
not matter,
not position,
not money,
not distance,
not time,
nothing, nothing
will come
between man and man,
between nation and nation.
The roots of separation
are already cut.
Wait to see
the drying of
the branches of
hatred,

and the leaves
of greed.
        It will take time,
        Brothers of darkness
        will try in vain
        to revitalize
        unrooted tree...
        their effort
        will teach them
        their failure.
Already
in the subtle
spheres of higher mind,
of great thinkers,
of great lovers,
of great creators,
the temple of humanity
is under
construction.
        Humanity found its way
        Home,
        through the way
        of right human relations,
        through the way
        of goodwill,
        sharing,
        tolerance,
        understanding,
        joy.
The workers are everywhere,
in all nations,
in all countries,
in all races.
        The great labor
        is going on
        and the temple of

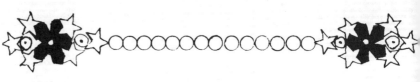

one humanity
is on its way
of construction.
Fiery engineers from
Shamballa are
watching the labor.
   "By human hands
   by human feet
   the temple will be
   built,"
where love
will prevail
and all men
will love.

The legend
says
in the year
2000
a great downflow of
the energy
of Shamballa
will take place
inaugurating the
age of
Aquarian beauty.
    Brother,
    do not worry,
    greater days are waiting for us.
    We cried long,
    we suffered long,
    but the age of joy
    is upon us.
        The age of great music,
        the age of divine architecture,
        the age of color and movement,
        the age of mysteries of initiation,
        the age of greater
        miracles of science
        is upon us.
Imagine!
The Masters of the Wisdom
once again
will walk
with man.
    They will demonstrate
    the power of mastery,

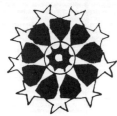

the beauty of life,
the joy of everlasting
progress,
the lightning of Infinity...
Imagine
the great One,
the Lord Christ
will appear
and will perform
the Initiation
ceremonies
in the temples of Masons,
in the Churches of faithful
and
in the
centers of great beauty.
The power of Shamballa
is cleansing
the path
to glory of human soul.
Man is a rare beauty.
There is a cosmos in him.
There is an Infinity in him.
There are unheard,
unseen
symphonies and
colors in him.
All these will come out gradually
as the great
Lord
will awaken us
in the mystery of initiations.
"It is the energy of
Shamballa
which prepares
the way

for the energy
of Hierarchy."
Cyclically
the energy of Shamballa
releases itself
into Hierarchy.
    And the legend says
    the members of Hierarchy
    often have
    hard time
    to adjust themselves
    to the voltage of
    the contact.
        Such a contact
        brings
        great changes
        in the plans and
        programming of the Hierarchy,
        changes of office,
        new initiations,
        new releases.
    Some of the members
    choose to go
    to the spheres of Higher
    Evolution.
As a result of these changes,
disciples from humanity
are initiated into Hierarchy.
    The methods of instruction
    and communication
    are changed,
    and greater responsibilities
    are given
    to the world disciples.
All Ashrams are
affected.

The instructions are brought
up-to-date,
in harmony
with the plan
and with the intentions
of the Lord
of the World.
    This life, my friend,
    is not a product
    of blind forces.
    "Nothing happens by
    accident."
    Great engineers are
    watching the labor
    of humanity,
    greater days of joy,
    of health,
    of prosperity
    are on the way.
        Do not have faith
        in prophesies
        which tell you
        the end of the world
        is near;
        tell you about
        the hopelessness
        of all good works, of all endeavor
        to bring peace, to spread goodwill;
        tell you about
        the savagery of human being.
        Do not have faith in them,
        they are the prophets of
        darkness.
Human spirit is always
victorious,
always it will be.

Humanity is a flowering
bush,
an opening lotus,
a rising star,
our destiny is in our
hands,
under the watchful
eyes of
the Captain of Shamballa.
    Spread the news of Joy,
    spread the ideas of
    one humanity,
    spread the ideas of
    brotherhood of angels and
    men.
        Sing,
      "The sons of men
        are one,
        I am one with them...
        Let vision come and insight.
        Let the future stand revealed.
        Let inner union demonstrate,
        outer cleavages be gone."
    Sing this song
    through your thoughts,
    through your writings,
    through your feelings,
    actions
    and relations...
        Let people hear you.
        Tell them
        The Christ is on His way.
        Tell them
        the dawn is just
        minutes away.
        Give them joy,

81

as only in joy
the vision is
understood,
and the labor
is carried on . . .
Rejoice!

The legend says;
Shamballa
has
three gifts for
humanity.
    One is *opportunity.*
    When the divine energy
    pours down
    it builds a
    bridge,
    a communication line
    between one whom it touches
    and the Door
    from which it
    emanates...
    It purifies
    and raises the fires of your
    being.
    It makes you to see yourself,
    your real face
    and the conditions of your life.
    It makes you
    To see the future, the vision...
    and thus opportunity comes to you,
    to surpass yourself,
    to leave behind
    the burdens of ages.
Opportunity comes to all men
to step forward
and to be born
again, in spirit,
or to pass the stream of purification,

83

or to climb
the mountain
of
transfiguration
in group formation.
Opportunity comes
to all initiates
to pass through
the fiery
sands of the deserts,
and
renounce
the pull of matter...
and break the chalice of oil
at the feet of
the Lord.
Opportunity comes
to all
victorious ones
to register
the call of Sirius
and become
a member
of Community
of the Brothers of humanity—
the Hierarchy,
and function
closer to the light
of Shamballa.
The call of
Shamballa is...
Proceed on the path
of self-exertion,
of labor,
of sacrifice
and the doors of higher realms

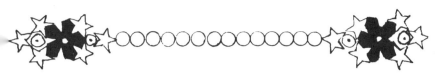

at this moment,
are waiting for your
footsteps.
Opportunity comes to all
nations,
to clean their homes,
to break the walls of
separation,
to build new bridges
of communication and dialogue,
to leave behind
old-age, worn out
systems of exploitation.
        The second gift
        is
        *enlightenment*
        the destruction of
        'avidya'—
        ignorance.
                Ignorance is identification,
                attachment,
                changing of polarity
                from positive to negative.
                Ignorance is
                zero
                communication
                with the
                life of the universe.
        Ignorance is
        bottling oneself
        and floating
        in
        the ocean.
Vidya
is
knowledge

which leads to
enlightenment.
    Knowledge is
    the growing light.
    You don't need to learn
    to know.
    You know because you unfold.
    You liberate,
    you release your
    Self.
Shamballa...
Salutations to you...
    The energy of Shamballa,
    the Lightning,
    gives *enlightenment*
    because
    it destroys age-long
    accumulations of
    darkness.
    It destroys the chains
    binding the Self to matter.
        *Enlightenment*...
        when all your lights
        on the Christmas tree
        of your Self
        are lit
        in their proper color
        and radiation,
        forming a chalice
        for the blessings
        of the Lord of Shamballa.
    Enlightenment
    is courage,
    is daring,
    is humility and endurance,
    it is gratitude,

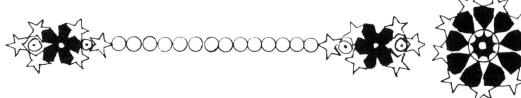

compassion,
simplicity,
serenity.
Enlightenment is the birth of the Soul,
Enlightenment is ability to see,
Enlightenment is the contact
with the greater Soul
in each
man.

There are
stages of enlightenment.
There are
personality,
soul
and spiritual enlightenments.
There are
planetary,
solar, galactic and cosmic
enlightenments.
Personality enlightenment is achieved
when man contacts
the Transpersonal Self
within,—
the inner Guide.

In this stage
the vehicles
of personality are purified gradually
and higher centers
absorb the energy
of lower ones.

In the second stage
of enlightenment
The human soul finds himself
and sees himself
as a Soul
infused with the splendour

of the inner
Guide.
  He becomes a shining beauty,
  a fountain of wisdom,
  in the world
  of men.
In the third stage
of enlightenment
the human soul
becomes
aware of himself as the
Self,
and masters all that is
not-self.
  At this stage
  He becomes a source of
  strength,
  enabling men to stand
  on the path.
  He becomes a source of
  creativity and leadership.
In planetary enlightenment, we are told,
his awareness
embraces
all kingdoms of nature.
  In Solar enlightenment
  his awareness
  embraces
  all centers
  functioning in the Solar
  ring-pass-not.
    In the next
    stage
    of enlightenment
    you enter
    into the awareness of the life

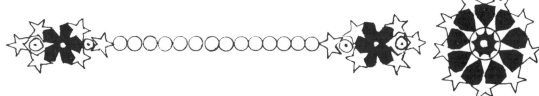

of the galaxy.
In the Cosmic Enlightenment
you enter
the freedom, the bliss
of
Space.

    In each enlightenment
    The Monad,
    the real you,
    as an eye,
    opens
    stage by stage
    and you become
    the all seeing
    Eye.
Enlightenment is the freedom
towards Infinity.
Enlightenment is ability
to bring Infinity
into your life—
To express Infinity
Through all you do.

    Gift of Shamballa...
    *Enlightenment*...
    we open our being,
    in all humility,
    aspiration
    and fiery striving
    to your gifts
    Shamballa.
The third gift of
Shamballa
*Brotherhood.*

    The energy of Shamballa
    is
    destructive

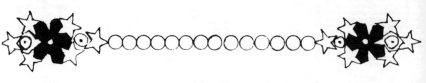

to all elements of
separatism.
It is destructive
to all those
who carry in their hearts
and minds
elements of hatred,
separatism,
selfishness.
As the Aquarian age
increases
its radiance
into the sphere of our world,
it will be
more and more
difficult
to contain hate and to be healthy,
to contain separative, selfish thoughts
and to be sane,
to have greed and
spirit of exploitation,
and
to be
creative.
The fire of Shamballa
will amplify
the energy of Aquarius
and rhythmically
will
strike
the earth.
        As a great hammer
        it will pave
        the way for the reappearance
        of the great Lord, Christ,
        Who

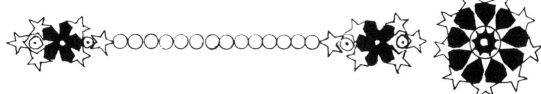

gave the command of the new age
"Love
one another,
as I love you...
There is no greater love
than the love
by which
a man
lays his life down
for his friends."
    This comment
    increasingly
    will
    be heard
    in the sanctuary
    of our soul
    and
    will
    create
    tolerance, forgiveness, sharing,
    cooperation,
    understanding
    and unity.
Shamballa, the Stronghold,
there is no
higher
gift
than the gift of
*Brotherhood*,
where the world
will be our home,
and every home
our garden.
Where people
will not hurt
each other.

Where all our resources
will not be
wasted
in crimes,
in wars,
in police force, in armies...
but
the resources will be used
for erecting
global institutions of
light,
great cathedrals
of science,
great theatres of
art.
        Still we will have
        a governing body,
        which will be
        a
        United Nations.
        The members of that body
        will be
        elected
        because
        they no longer need recognition,
        they no longer need money,
        they no longer
        have
        the craving
        to be glorified.
        They will be
        persons,
        who
        are able to live
        within the vision
        of the great

observing eye
of the Lord
of Shamballa.
  They will be people in direct contact
  with
  the ruling department
  of the
  Hierarchy.
They will present
a vision,
a plan
for progressive
unfoldment
of the human
psyche,
so that
man,
tunes in
to greater capacity
with the system of
Cosmos.
Thus the purpose of the
great Lord
will guide
the little wills of men
in a
great
symphonic beauty.
  Only after
  Brotherhood,
  humanity
  as a center
  in our
  Solar system,
  will make the first contact
  with the other

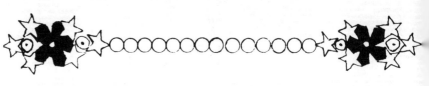

evolutions in our own
galaxy.
Man will be able
to recognize
himself
in other human beings.
Suffering and pain
will no longer
be
the teachers of humanity.
Joy and striving
will replace them.
Joy is greater than knowledge.
Joy is wisdom.
Opportunity,
enlightenment,
Brotherhood;
three gifts of Shamballa
in the Aquarian age.
Those who strive
need not to wait
on the path of time,
the gifts are there
already.
With intense striving,
leaving behind your old self,
with motive
pure and divine,
approach the sanctuary
of your inner Self
and the gifts
are there.
Take the gift of *opportunity*
and today
decide to be harmless,
giving,

self-forgetful,
joyful,
universal—forever.
And you already are
in the process
of unwrapping
your gift.
     Man in his essence
     is the *opportunity,*
     an open way
     towards Infinity.
Take the gift *enlightenment*
and today
think, feel and act
in the light
of the great Presence
in your
inner universe.
     Decide to see
     things as they are.
     Change the angles
     of your observation.
     Try to see the happenings in the world.
     Try to see every event,
     not only through your own eyes
     but through the eyes
     of so-called
     enemies.
     Multiply your vision
     and
     do not live
     only for yourself,
     only for your nation,
     only for your religion,
     but for entire
     *humanity.*

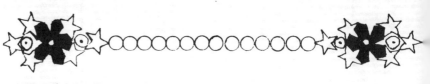

And every day,
before sunrise
raise your soul
to the Light Supernal
in meditation.
Thus,
your light will increase
and
eventually you
will unwrap your
second gift.
    Stretch your hand
    take the
    gift
    of *Brotherhood.*
Every day think, feel and act
as if all human beings
were
your
beloved brothers.
Never, never express any word that
hurts them
and
creates disunity.
    Never, never
    hold your self,
    or your race,
    or your nation
    above the interest of humanity.
Give opportunity
to everyone
to shine his light.
Give light
to everyone,
to see the oneness of
the souls of

men.
> Then
> you, as a brother of men,
> will
> lead
> humanity
> towards
> the age of Aquarius,
> in which
> man is the keeper of
> his brother,
> in which
> joy is the daily sunshine,
> and striving
> towards the Supreme
> is the labor
> of everyone.

Shamballa,
Shamballa,
resplendent center of power;
Glory to you!
Gratitude to you!
> What would be our destiny
> without
> Shamballa?
> A dark night
> in the ocean,
> without
> a compass
> without a beacon,
> without hope
> of a sunrise.

Shamballa!
Shamballa!
We bring our hearts
to your altar

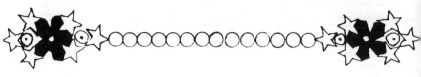

and give our word
to strive,
labor,
and sacrifice
on the path to eternity.

Legends are more real
than history.
Legends
speak to us
about the world of causes,
about
blueprints,
prototypes.
    Events are the faint echoes
    of a cause.
    Events develop
    an external observation,
    legends develop
    an
    internal observation.
    They are not
    impeded
    by time, location and national interests.
    Thus
    the legends
    are direct ways of communication
    with the world of causes.
    The legend says:
   "Peace
    is
    the expression of the will
    of Shamballa.
    It produces
    balance,
    equilibrium,
    synthesis
    and understanding.

It produces
a spirit of invocation
and evocation..."
Invocation is
the strong demand, the will
of the human soul,
the fiery love of the human heart
and the radiating light
of the human being;
as a flash of lightning
it reaches
Shamballa
and
evokes
response from It.
    As one thus contacts
    Shamballa,
    peace will be with him.
    Peace will overflow through him,
    he will evoke peace
    wherever his eyes touch...
        "Peace be with you..."
    I give my peace to you...
    Blessed are those
    who make peace,
        they are the children of the Most High.
Peace cannot be established
by force of the armies,
by the forces of fear, promises and bribery,
by the forces of pain and suffering.
We tried all these
all over the world
and peace is not yet here.
    Peace can be established
    only when
    the little wills of men

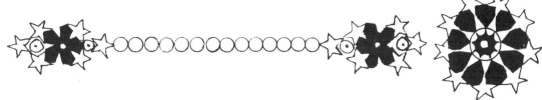

touch the peace of Shamballa
when cyclically
it pours down
its fiery
bliss.
Peace is energy,
communion,
decentralization of self.
Peace is love,
unmoved
by any circumstance,
in any condition.
Whenever you touch
the fiery field of
Shamballa,
peace
descends in you,
or peace
blooms in you.
Only by increasing peace
the purpose of Shamballa
is revealed to you;
the purpose of the Captain
of the earth-ship
will be known by you.
The purpose in Shamballa
is the
focussed will of Solar Lord.
The will of the Solar Lord
is
one of the notes of the symphony
of the Lord,
whose body is the
galaxy as a whole.
Salutations,
adoration

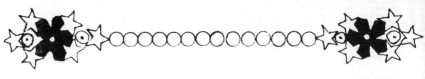

and glory
to Him!
Peace! Peace! Peace!
    "Peace is
        the expression
        of the will
        of
        Shamballa."

Shamballa is an open,
fiery Lotus
of thousand petals.
Each petal
a receiver, accumulator
and transmitter.
Energies from Venus, Pluto,
from Solar Entities,
from the Great Bear,
Pleiades
and Taurus,
pour into the chalice
of Shamballa.
    Shamballa absorbs them,
    transforms them
    with the purpose
    and power.
    This is the force
    that
    is released cyclically
    upon the world,
    as a lightning,
    as an opportunity, enlightenment,
    Brotherhood.
Each entity
in Shamballa
is a vortex of energy,
is a fiery
commander of forces of light.
Each entity
is a web of communication
with Cosmos.

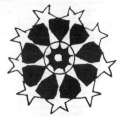

Shamballa is a magnet,
the pull of which
is felt
in the heart
of each initiate.
Initiate is a man
whose vehicles
of expression
are purified
with the fire of the heart.
Three great
energies emanate from
Shamballa, the Seat of Fire;
the energy of *purification*
is the first.
This energy
purifies
all vehicles of man
in greater and greater and greater
transmutation,
until the bodies are transformed
and
transfiguration is achieved.
Through a transfigured
personality or substance,
the spirit
can
manifest itself unobscured.
This energy
for all humanity,
for all kingdoms
opens the path
of greater
fusion
with the spirit.
The second energy

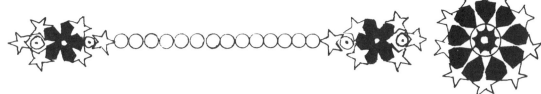

is
the energy
of *destruction*.
　　"It removes the forms
　　which are
　　imprisoning
　　the inner
　　spiritual life;
　　under
　　cyclic law
　　this destructive energy
　　comes into play
　　and destroys the forms of life
　　which
　　prevent
　　divine expression."
This energy
is under the control
of the
Council of Shamballa.
It is also brought into activity
by the free wills of men
to meet the needs
of new cycles
or to get free
from the prison
of old forms.
　　The third energy is
　　the
　　energy
　　of
　　*organization*.
Whenever the Shamballa energy
is released,
there is purification.
There is destruction.

There is organization.
    Organization is the process
    of adaptation of life
    to the Plan,
    harmonization of the life
    to the
    purpose of the Lord,
    and
    the labor
    to carry on the torch
    of Shamballa.
All these three energies
first
act
on the subtle planes,
then slowly
manifest themselves
on the physical
plane.
    Shamballa energy
    purifies
    the mental sphere of humanity,
    making it
    more sensitive
    to the lights of intuition,
    to the joy of Soul,
    to the visions of higher worlds.
        Shamballa energy
        destroys,
        burns away
        age-long crystallizations,
        age-long distortions,
        heavy clouds of hatred,
        thoughts of separation,
        greed
        and

106

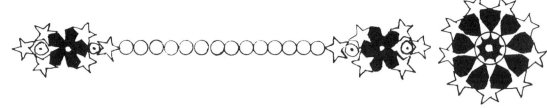

crime,
and gives opportunity for man
to try again
the path leading
to the summit.
Shamballa energy
organizes
the souls of the New Age
for greater
group endeavors,
for greater humanitarian
service,
for greater focus and tension
to contact
the lights of the destiny
of divine
spark.
Shamballa energy
bridges the gaps,
and man
comes in contact
with the Future...
Shamballa is the Future of
those who
labor
"with their hands and
feet."
Shamballa is the
state of consciousness,
state of awareness,
to which the soul of
all humanity is striving.

The increase of righteousness,
The increase of love
and brotherhood,
The increase of freedom,
can be measured
by the endeavour
of the dark forces to appose
love, brotherhood, freedom
and righteousness.
At this time
the dark Lodge
is trying to increase
The fire of hatred,
The fire for possession,
The fire of separation.
 Today this fire
 is aimed
 at the destruction
 of human race.
The forces of darkness
are planning
to use this fire
to wipe away
the culture
of the àges,
bringing death
to human kingdom
and turn
this planet into
a frozen
moon.
 They dream this can be the destruction

of the human race
and the victory
of the dark
lodge—
which works
through
greed, hatred and fear—
and is anxious
to establish
in the world
as many agents,
as many stations
possible,
to retard
the evolution
of humanity.
They dream to retard
The evolution of humanity
millions of years
using the methods of destruction
of their agents,
to turn mother earth
into ashes
to such a degree
that
it may not be able
to provide
bodies
for waiting souls
for millions of years.
This is the dream of the dark lodge.
    Shamballa energy
    is the fire
    That
    annihilates such dreams,
    such a desire of dark forces

109

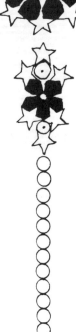

by strengthening
the flame of spirit in every man.
This fire, this flame of spirit
"must be
distributed
and
used effectively
by the disciples
of great Ones..."
"This fire
in reality
is the fire
of
the will-to-love.
Not love alone
but
will-to-love."
A love that
streams forth
from your essence,
and as a fire
burns away
motives
based
on greed, fear, hatred.
Such a love
may take you
to the fields of great suffering,
to the spheres
of burning fire,
but the disciple
of the great Ones
walks on them
with a song in his heart,
with
faith immovable

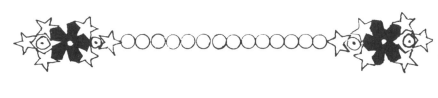

in his soul,
with
the love that puts
his life
for his
friends.
This fire
of
the will-to-love
can be
kindled with flame,
touching
the
fire of Shamballa.
Those who touch
the fire
of Shamballa
and
assimilate it through
their sacrificial
life
and will-to-love
become
the messengers of fire
supernal,
who gradually and eventually
set
aflame
all hearts
that have
a drop
of love and vision in them
for humanity.
Thus
the Lord's army
will

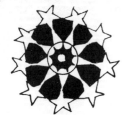

organize and grow
and follow
the Commander
on the
white horse.
       From East to West,
       from North to South
       in all
       humanity,
       the knights of spirit
       will bring their
       torch
       and join
       the army of the Lord.
They will have weapons,
but
the weapons
of love, of beauty,
of will-to-love,
simplicity,
sincerity,
detachment
and the
light of intuition.
       Nothing, nothing
       will be able to resist them.
       The fire of
       Shamballa will strike
       every obstacle
       on its path
       of global Brotherhood.
Shamballa,
Shamballa,
our north star,
our beacon on the stormy sea,
our Home, our Refuge.

The liberation of humanity
is in the hands
of seven groups.
   *"The men and women of goodwill"*
   who
   will good
   to all men.
   They act, they feel, they think
   in the terms of good,
   and they put into action
   the goodness
   they have in their hearts.
   *"The idealists, the visionaries of a*
   *future world"*
   Who,
   dream a better world,
   who conceive in their thoughts
   the world of future,
   a new world,
   not a future, the result of past,
   but a future, planned on the purpose divine,
   in which
   man is able to reach
   his highest.
The vision of the future,
a future world
can be a source of inspiration
to world leader
and to
humanity as a whole.
      Then we have *"world aspirants"*
      who are turning their faces

113

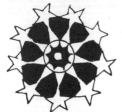

to the
Seat of fire
trying to purify,
to organize,
to enlighten
the vehicles
of the inner
fire—
Who, one by one
breaking
the chains
of their feet—
Who, day after day
are looking into
greater
horizons—
By their examples, they will teach
the inner path.
Next there are disciples
throughout the planet,
who are in contact
consciously
with their inner Guide,
who are in contact
with
the Masters of their Soul
who see
the Plan
and
strive to live a life
to manifest
the Plan
of the great fiery Ones.
They walk
on the Rainbow
and express

114

the music of the Plan
in all they do,
in all they are.
They sacrifice,
they renounce,
they persist.
The next group is
"The members of the spiritual Hierarchy"
the liberated
Ones,
those who conquered death,
time, space,
Those who are
in closer contact
with the
Seat of Fire,
Those who serve
the Purpose
of the Lord.
    Our gratitude
    as incense
    of thousand altars
    rises to Them.
        Those Who
        throughout ages,
        protected the human race,
        through light,
        love,
        goodness,
        simplicity,
        beauty,
        and truth.
        Glory to Them
        who stand by humanity!
Next we have
"The custodians

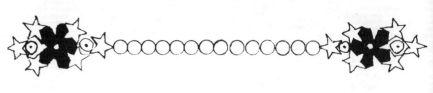

of the will
or purpose
of God."
    The flames in Shamballa,
    who
    are ready
    to strike
    the lightning
    and
    clear
    the way for humanity
    as
    the will-to-love
    grows
    and knocks at the gates of
    Shamballa.
  "Search and you will find.
  Knock and it will be opened,
  ask and you will receive,"
  said
  the human
  Representative in Shamballa.
  Then we have
 "Certain great energies
 Extra-planetary,
 Who stand ready
 to intervene
 should the spiritual invocation
 or the distress
 of humanity
 reach
 the pitch
 of evocation."
    That is why
    Christ
    the Lord

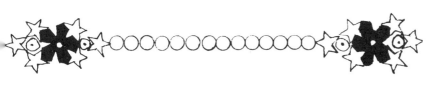

in 1945
June Full Moon,
gave us
*The Great
Invocation.*
"From the point of Light
within the Mind of God
Let light stream forth into
the minds of men.
Let light descend on Earth.
From the point of Love
within the heart of God
Let love stream forth into
the hearts of men.
May Christ return to earth.
From the centre where the
will of God is known
Let purpose guide the little
wills of men—
The purpose which the
Masters know and
serve.
From the centre which we
call the race of men
Let the Plan of Love and
Light work out.
And may it seal the door
where evil dwells.
Let Light and Love and
Power restore the Plan
on Earth."
        This invocation
        will prevent
        any war
        black forces may contemplate,
        if sounded

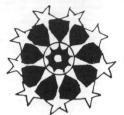

in greater intensity
by greater number of people
everywhere.
　　This invocation
　　will evoke the attention
　　of great Lives,
　　Who
　　will intervene,
　　and carry on
　　the battle
　　for us
　　on higher planes
　　until
　　the darkness
　　is
　　defeated in its home—
　　destroyed
　　under
　　the feet of forces of light
　　and cast out of the planet.
This great Invocation
will build the Path
of the return of Christ
with
all
His
disciples
and will establish
the mysteries
of Initiation.
He will teach us
the science of immortality,
Karma
and
the science of rebirth.
　　He will teach us

118

how to contact
the Stronghold.
He will teach us
the Science of Contact
with greater
and greater
realities.
He will teach us
how to renounce,
how to sacrifice,
how
to initiate ourselves
into the
path of
Resurrection.
    In olden days
crucifixion
was emphasized in all our
ceremonies.
In this age of Aquarius,
He will
inaugurate
the age of Resurrection
and
will teach
the science of Resurrection
to humanity.
    He will bring with Him,
great Angels
Who
throughout ages
watched
the steps of
humanity
and protected the people
when

the dark nights
came
upon
them.
The order is
given to Him
by Father
to transform this planet
into
a sacred
planet,
and that is what
He is doing
all these thousands of years.
Inspiring, encouraging
every flame of love,
every flame of light,
every flame of will-to-good
in every heart
of man,
so that
at the end of Aquarian
Age
He has humanity
at the
gate of greater initiation
and
the planet
transformed into a sacred
planet.
A planet
where no crime
can be committed anymore.
A planet,
the citizens of which
are

embodiments
of love,
knowledge,
sacrifice,
beauty and health.
    A planet,
    where the purpose of Lord
    will guide
    the little wills of men,
    the purpose which the Masters
    know
    and serve.
The legend says;
Christ,
because of His
unparalleled achievement,
for the first time
in history
contacted a Solar agency
Whose name is
the Spirit of Peace.
Great Lord Buddha
established
the first major contact
with the Forces of Light.
    Since then
    every full moon of Taurus,
    these two energies
    pour down
    upon humanity
    to create right human relations,
    enlightenment,
    understanding,
    and
    peace and power
    as far as humanity can

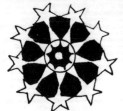

respond.
   Peace
   is not
   a condition in the world.
   It is energy
   which creates right human relations,
   harmonizes,
   aligns the human and planetary
   centers,
   releases inner beauty
   and impresses the will of the Mighty C
   in your heart.
This energy can be absorbed
and
utilized
by the unfolding petals
of the heart.
Those who have open hearts
now
can contact this energy
and
spread the symphony
of peace.
Peace
leads to attunement with
Cosmos.

Shamballa
has Its messengers,
the great Avatars
Who can only be contacted
on the higher mental plane.
　　"They embody divine purpose,
　　　the energy pouring through Them
　　　and transmitted by Them
　　　is focussed
　　　through the Lord of the World.
　　　　"They can only be reached
　　　　　by the united voices of
　　　　　the Hierarchy and of
　　　　　humanity.
　　　　　Speaking in unison,
　　　　　Their service is evoked only
　　　　　by realized need
　　　　　and only after those who call
　　　　　Them forth
　　　　　have added to their faith
　　　　　strenuous action

and have done their utmost,
alone and unaided,
to overcome evil."
"They occasionally
reach those thinking people,
focussed on mental planes,
who have clear vision,
potent resolve,
directed will
and open minds
plus, essential purity of form.
"These Avatars
express the will of the Solar Lord,
the energy of Shamballa
and the impulse
lying behind divine purpose."
When They come forth
They bring destruction first,
and death
to all limiting forms
and forms that house the evil.
And thus reveal, the purpose
of the great, great Lord.
This is why meditation,
mental polarization
and Invocation,
are urgent
to seal the door where evil
dwells...
To seal the door
by the power of the great Messengers
and
by the power of
focussed will-to-good
of humanity,
which

evokes the energy of Shamballa
and contacts
the Avatars of the Most High.

There are
The major full moons
When the Lord Christ
becomes the recipient
of energies
From Shamballa
to relate humanity
to Hierarchy,
The Hierarchy to Shamballa.
　　At the full moon
　　of Aries
　　Christ makes
　　closer contact
　　with the Spirit of Resurrection,
　　a great living Entity
　　in the Council
　　at Shamballa.
　　This helps Him
　　to draw closer the spirit
　　of man
　　towards the Eternal Youth.
　　　　At the time
　　　　of Aries Full Moon
　　The spirit of man
　　receives a call
　　for resurrection.
　　　　Many Sons of man
　　　　hear this call
　　　　and they
　　　　submit themselves

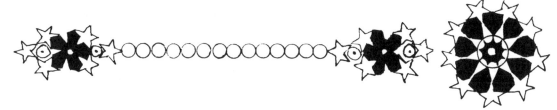

to a greater discipline,
to a greater service
and sacrifice....
To raise themselves
from the physical,
emotional and mental limitations
and enter
into the plane of freedom
and joy.
"The secret of Aries
is the secret
of beginnings,
of cycles,
and of emerging
opportunities."
At the Full Moon
of Taurus
The great Lord,
Christ,
with the Lord of
Compassion
The Buddha,
and with the Lord of the World at Shamballa
create
a Triangle of Light.
This light is released
at the Full Moon
of Gemini
to all humanity.
The Lord of the World
is the light of Life.
The Lord Buddha is the Lord
of Wisdom,
revealing the purpose to Hierarchy.
The Christ, the Lord of Love
representing, the demand of humanity

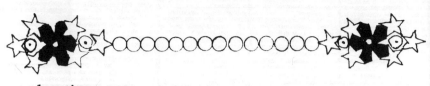

and acting
as the distributing
agent
for the forces of Enlightenment.
    The forces of Enlightenment
    will increase
    day after day
    in such a degree
    that
    man
    will be able to see
    his eternal Future
    and recognize
    the obstacles
    on his path.
At the Taurus Full Moon
The released energies
will stimulate
the Spirit of Love,
The Spirit of brotherhood
and goodwill
on the earth.
"They will fuse
all men of goodwill
into
an
integrated,
responsive whole."
    The legend commands
    That
    on each Full Moon
    of Taurus
    We rededicate
    ourselves
    to the will of God.
The next full moon
is the Full Moon of Gemini.

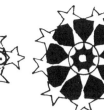

At this Full Moon
of Gemini
Christ, the great Lord,
gathers
into Himself
the united Invocation of
humanity,
the prayers, the demand
of humanity,
and transmits it
to Shamballa.
　　This is why
　　every man
　　in the month of Gemini
　　must focus himself
　　on the spirit of Christ
　　and live in Him
　　with all his heart
　　and with
　　all his being.
The Full Moon of Gemini
is that moment
when the Heart of the Sun
pours out
the river of love
which
Christ
carries out to all men;
He is the Aquarius on the planet.
　　At this full moon
　　He stands
　　in Shamballa as the Representative
　　of the human race
　　and bridges
　　humanity with the
　　intent of
　　Shamballa.

129

The great, great Lord,
the Soul of this planet,
the living, acting
planetary Logos
is in process of greater Initiation.
This puts
greater pressure
upon three centers;
humanity, Hierarchy, Shamballa.
As the great Man
in the heavens, the planetary Logos
proceeds
on His path of expansion,
initiation,
He fuses with the sources
of greater energy,
and charges His three Centers
with greater energy.
The three centers
respond
according to the unfoldment
of their own members
and a new striving,
self-exertion
towards the path of perfection

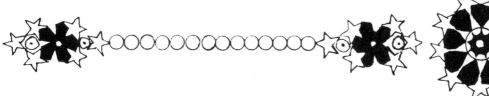

awakens in them.
The Heavenly Man,
as a Magnet,
pulls up the living Spark
in the hearts of the members
of each Center.
    This process of greater,
    greater response, creates
    greater friction in the human center,
    and new ways
    of progress,
    conflict,
    problems,
    and even
    greater destruction
    of limiting forms on three levels...
In Hierarchy
greater activity to adjust
to the incoming energies
and reconsideration
of the Plan.
    Nothing exists obsolete
    in the Center of the Masters,
    in the great Community of Holy Ones.
        Hierarchy
        endeavors to adjust Itself to Shamballa
        and relate all changes
        to humanity.
    These changes penetrate
    into each Ashram
    of the Masters
    into each group of Their Disciples.
        These changes involve
        the discipline which They
        go through
        for Their relation with Shamballa.

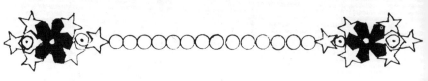

Hierarchy is the Heart Center
of the Logos.
Because of His advancement
greater love pours down
from the petals of the Hierarchy
to humanity.
　　　Love energy
　　　creates
　　　group activity, relationships,
　　　greater understanding, reorientation
　　　and also friction
　　　between expanding and contracting forces
　　　in man,
　　　in planet.
Shamballa
goes through greater tension
at this time of greater Initiation
of the great
Heavenly Man.
　　　"It involves
　　　the ability of Those
　　　in the Council Chamber
　　　at Shamballa
　　　to react to
　　　and absorb
　　　certain extra-planetary
　　　energies
　　　and use them to
　　　an intra-planetary sense."
The Legend says
the Heavenly Man
on His path of Initiation,
is running faster
than was expected
by the Great Observers
in the system.

This is why
the atom,
the man, the Hierarchy and Shamballa
are in the process of release,
are in process
of readjustment, unfoldment and blooming.
>This is why
>humanity coming together
>in greater group action.
>Aspirants of the world
>are eager to know about the Hierarchy,
>and disciples of the world
>are anxious
>to make a contact
>with Shamballa.
A golden Bridge
is uniting
these three centers
for greater cooperation.
>The Brothers of humanity
>have faith
>on the soundness
>of the heart
>of humanity.
The prisoner of the planet
is in process
of becoming
free...
And this is the great opportunity
for all units,
to proceed into greater glory.
Never in the history of humanity,
we are told
the door of initiation
was wider open.
>Many hundreds

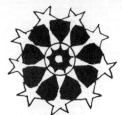
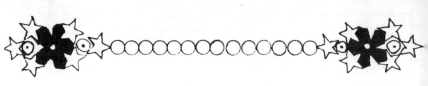

are approaching the mountain
of transfiguration.
Many thousands are passing
through the stream of purification.
Many millions
are going through birth pains...
And few here and there
are making greater
contact with Hierarchy
and Shamballa.
The members of the Hierarchy
have Their day of opportunity.
Some of Them
are entering
into the path of Higher Evolution
and one by one,
They are leaving our planet,
as humans
are replacing Them.
The stream of light from Logos
to human heart is glowing in beauty,
and pearls of soul
are travelling
to the heart of the Sun.
The legend says,
"Such an awakening
of human family,
such a major spiritual
reorientation
was unexpected
until 4500 A.D.
when
our Sun will enter
into the sign of
Capricorn."
Humanity went ahead

2000 years in its evolution.
Do not listen
the voices
of pseudo prophets
who
because of their blindness
can not see the light,
can not see
the coming glory of humanity
and the world.
The great Teacher
Master Djwhal Khul
says,
"The work of the Hierarchy,
throughout the ages
has been fundamentally threefold
in nature.
A constant effort to set up
a closer and more understanding
relation with Shamballa.
This involves
an unfoldment of the will aspect
in conjunction with a full use
of intelligent love;
A constant adaptation
of the developing Plan
to the emerging,
energising Purpose;
an increasing ability
to transmit energy
from Shamballa
to the three worlds,
from the Cosmic etheric levels
to the Cosmic
dense physical planes.
"To unfold—within

the periphery of the
hierarchical center—
a life, a plan
and a technique
which will train all who
find
their way into an Ashram.
(into the subjective
class of a great One.)
"To represent within the Hierarchy
the qualities of all Seven Rays
through the medium
of the seven major Ashrams
and their allied and subsidiary
Ashrams."
The goal of the Hierarchy
is to link
humanity with Shamballa.
As the goal of Soul
is to link
personality with the Spark.
The goal of the Hierarchy
is to be absorbed in Shamballa
and in
humanity.
And as this progress goes on,
we will see
that Hierarchy will slowly
disappear
and only two centers
will remain—
Shamballa and humanity.
Symbolically
the Hierarchy
will be resurrected into
Shamballa

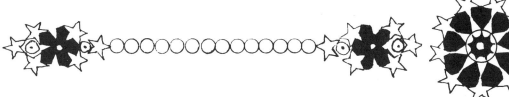

and humanity will come
in direct continuous contact
with the seat of Fire.
   The preparatory step
   of such an event is
   the externalization
   of the Hierarchy
   and
   the reappearance of Christ.
      Lord Christ
      will build the permanent road
      between humanity and Shamballa.
      This labor
      will mark
      the completion of His major Initiation,
Resurrection.
         Thus the temporary Center,
         The Hierarchy,
         as causal body
         of the Initiate of Renunciation,
         will exist
         no more.
         This will be also
         the great
         defeat for dark forces
         on the planet.

Shamballa,
the great Lotus,
records impressions
coming from
great space . . .
        As the Captain of the Ship
        is in contact
        with various
        guiding stations
        on the shores and at sea.
There are many
Cosmic dangers:
dangers from
disintegrating planets,
moons,
comets, constellations,
electrical storms,
floods of energy in space,
tidal waves
of forces created by
earthquakes
within great deserts
of energy fields
in Solar and Cosmic spheres.
There are explosions
of energy accumulations
in space.
        Our earth
        and other planets,
        and systems, are little boats
        on the ocean
        of the living, mighty

138

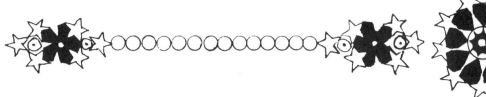

waves of space.
The Captain of our boat
is on duty
twenty four hours,
millions of years,
to lead
the boat to the destined shore
of the future perfections.
        The communication system
        is Shamballa,
        the great Lord and His Council.
They contact
distant stars
such as Sirius
and receive impressions
from the great Lodge
on Sirius.
        The legend says
        these impressions are so subtle
        that the great lives in Shamballa
        must go through a special
        preparation,
        and with the presence
        of entire Council
        receive the message
        from Sirius.
                Sirius may inform them
                about
                events going on
                on higher levels
                which may affect
                the planet earth, its present and future.
                After the impression is received
                the whole Council
                is occupied
                to utilize the message

139

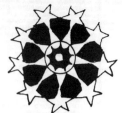
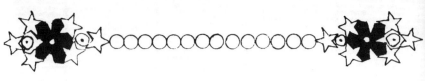

for the Hierarchy,
for humanity,
for other kingdoms,
and direct accordingly
the distribution of energy.
Shamballa receives
impressions
also from
the Great Bear, from Taurus,
from Pleiades,
and from other
constellations
when
they are cyclically
en rapport
with our
planet;
impressions concerning
spiritual events
in higher spheres,
impressions concerning
Cosmic plans and education,
impressions concerning
the secrets of electricity,
fire and matter in the great galaxy.
The legend says
such impressions
reach Shamballa
when ·
the great Council
is sitting in conclave
with a majority
of its members present...
Impressions also received
from
energy centers on two planets

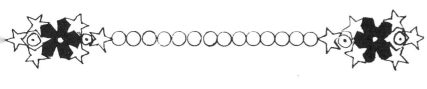

which cyclically
form a triangular
relationship
with our planet.
These impressions are received
by the three great
Buddhas of Activity
in Shamballa
and transmitted
to Hierarchy
for consideration
in planning
and activity.
    Impressions are
    received further
    from Venus.
    Venus is
    the higher
    Self
    of our planet.
    The Legend says,
    these impressions are
    received
    by Sanat Kumara
    and by three of His Council,
    Who
    are chosen by Him,
    any specific time,
    to act as recipients.
The whole Cosmos is
the source of impressions.
And as we grow
our contact will expand
into Infinity.
    The whole Existence
    is in contact

in many levels,
in many ways.
Only the awareness
of this contact
must be developed
by every life.
It is the development
of this awareness
that carries us
towards unity,
towards synthesis,
on individual
and
cosmic scales.
All those who graduate
from the
school of experiment,
will enter
into the course
of the supreme science
of contact.
The salvation of all systems,
the liberation
of each life
is achieved
through the science
of contact.
Lack of the knowledge
of this science
is the cause
of all distortions,
of all
pains and frictions.
Initiation into mysteries
is only possible
through the knowledge

of the science
of
contact.
This is why we are told
to love,
to understand,
to be sensitive,
to build our communication system,
the Rainbow Bridge.
    Those who build the bridge
    between themselves and
    their souls
    come closer to each other
    and form
    enlightened groups,
    and then
    try to build
    in group formation
    the higher part of the bridge,
    which extends
    from the soul
    to the Spark
    within man.
As groups build
such a bridge,
they get closer to each other
and present
a mighty source
of willpower,
of love energy,
and streams of light
for humanity.
    This is how humanity is united,
    not by force,
    but by achievement of contact
    with higher levels

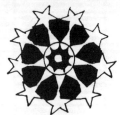
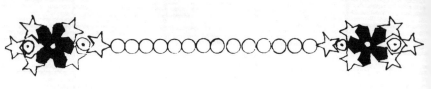

of existence.
We have communicating agents
between
galaxy and Solar System,
between Solar System
and Shamballa,
between Shamballa
and Hierarchy,
between the Hierarchy
and humanity
and
between nations and nations,
between man and man
and so on.
    My friend
    we are not alone
    in this universe.
    We are a part of it.
    We have a role to play,
    We have
    responsibility
    in this great symphony of
    Cosmos.
Shamballa
receives impressions
but also
emanates impressions
"In great cycles, and cyclic waves.
These are impulsed
from
extra-planetary sources,
as demanded or invoked
by the Lord of the World
and His
associates.
They emanate in response to

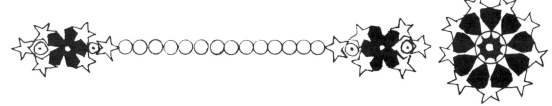

the acclaimed will
of Sanat Kumara
in the Council Chamber.
    These impressions,
    spiritual and ultimate,
    move outward
    along seven rays,
    as seven streams
    of spiritual energy,
    qualified and colored
    by the Shamballa
    impression.
        This process repeats itself
        when hierarchical invocation
        is effective
        and successfully established.
            The same
            process is repeated
            between Hierarchy and humanity
            in response
            to human invocation."
Shamballa
impresses the Hierarchy
through great Beings
Who are called
Nirmanakayas.
    Thus the Hierarchy
    is kept aware
    of changes in Shamballa,
    to plan
    accordingly.
        These impressions
        are passed
        to humanity
        through
        the New Group

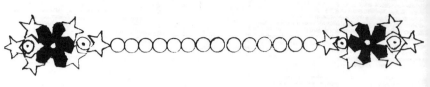

of World
Servers
so that
humanity as a whole
may tune itself
with the plan
of Hierarchy,
with the purpose
of Shamballa,
in accordance
with the greater
intent in galaxy.
Once a closer and
a purer relationship
is established
between these
great Centers,
the divine Life
will circulate
more freely
and bring
to all Centers
greater joy, greater bliss,
greater glory.
Shamballa,
Shamballa,
may your light
always shine
on the path
of humanity.

The legend says
more and more
sons of men
will stand in greater light
and pass through
major initiations.
    They will be able
    to transfigure
    their vehicles,
    enter into the great
    and lonely path
    of renunciation,
    stand in the supreme light
    of Revelation.
All this progress
of human soul
makes man
sensitive
progressively
to the impressions
of Shamballa.
Eventually
the four gates
and three doors of Shamballa
are entered,
and man stands in his age-long
golden dream,
to be a living golden pillar
in the Temple
of Father's Home.
    The pillar is the symbol
    of receiver
    of divine will and Purpose.

147

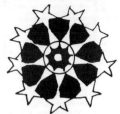

"Purpose
emanates
from the Cosmic
mental plane
and is
all inclusive,
synthetic,
motivating principle,
which
expresses itself
as
the divine will
upon the cosmic physical plane,
the seven planes
of our
planetary life."
This dynamic energy
focuses
itself in the
living, mighty pillars
at Shamballa.
Pillars also
are the symbols
of the golden
Rainbow Bridge.
Antahkarana...
through which
man achieves the other Shore
of divine
Beauty.
Morya Sahib
once stated,
"The universal
Eye of Shamballa
brings bliss to mankind.
The universal

148

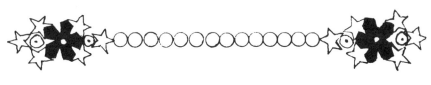

Eye of Shamballa
is a light
on the
path of mankind.
The universal Eye
of Shamballa
is the Star
which has guided
all seekers....
      The Ruler of Shamballa
      is a fiery
      Impeller
      of Life and Fire,
      His breath
      is ablaze with flame
      and His heart
      is aglow with Fire
      of the silvery Lotus.
      The Ruler of Shamballa
      lives
      and breathes
      in the Heart of the Sun.
The Ruler of Shamballa
is invincible
turning destruction into construction.
Accept
the Ruler of Shamballa
as the
manifestation of Life.
Thrice I say
of Life,
because Shamballa
is the guarantee
of human
aspirations..."
      "The Ruler of Shamballa

manifests
three covenants to humanity.
The Teaching
manifested by Maitreya (the Christ)
summons
the human spirit to Our Creative World.
The
Teaching of Maitreya
ordains
the Infinite in Cosmos, in life
and in the attainments of the spirit.
The Teaching
of Maitreya guards
the knowledge
of the Cosmic Fire
as the
unfoldment of the heart,
which embraces
the manifestation of the Universe.
The ancient legend
that affirms the
manifestation of Maitreya
as a resurrection of the spirit
is correct.
    The resurrection
    of the spirit,
    as conscious acceptance
    of the Teaching of Maitreya
    may be
    precursor of the Advent.
    Verily the resurrection.''

Shamballa,
the nine pointed
Diamond Star...
Nine-sided pyramid in the ether,
the sphere of fire, reflected
in the hearts of those
who tread the Path...
Each one
holding
the symbol of evolution,
the triangle.
There are those
who work hard
through the power of Invocation,
to transmute
the substance
of the etheric formations
on the planet
using the fire of light.
 Thus the etheric square patterns
 of the energy circulation
 of the planet
 consciously began to change
 into
 triangular formations.
 This is the Triangle of Light.
  There are those
  who work hard
  to form triangles of goodwill
  through which
  the goodness, beauty
  and the spirit

of sharing
can circulate;
radiating
fiery blessings everywhere,
forming networks of
light and goodwill
and creating
right human relations.
More advanced
sons of light
and goodwill
are forming
triangle
the third.
This triangle
is triangle
of Will,
through which
Will energy,
qualified with
purpose divine,
is
in circulation
from one point to another.
　　　Thus light
　　　and love
　　　and power
　　　are in action to bring
　　　changes
　　　on earth.
Shamballa is the source of true light,
is the source of pure love,
is the source of purpose and power.
　　　These energies
　　　must manifest in triangular formation,
　　　first with three individuals

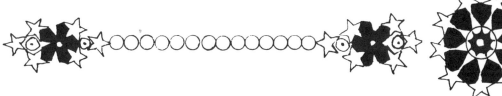

than three groups,
than three nations—
working first
as seeds,
then
multiplying into
many triangles
until the energies of Shamballa
are circulated
only
in the pattern
of triangles.
In a new age,
humanity will try
to change
the triangular pattern
built in the etheric body
of the planet
into circles,
concentric circles,
the center of which
will be
Shamballa.
The pulsations of Shamballa,
wave after wave
will reach
all kingdoms
through human circles
centered
in Shamballa.
The pulsations of Shamballa
will radiate
light,
love,
will,
creating in each circle

beauty,
joy
and bliss.
This is how
humanity step by step
will go
from
glory to glory.

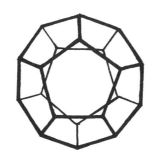

In Shamballa
is hidden
the Rod of Christ,
the world Teacher.
   On each end of this Rod
   There is a large diamond knob
   which
   radiates energy
   and colors, orange and blue.
   This is His Rod of Power.
      It is
      charged
      by the "flaming diamond"—
      the Rod
      of the Sanat Kumara,
      the Ancient of Days.
The legend says,
a wonderful
ceremony is performed
at the time
that
a new world Teacher
takes up His work.
During the ceremony
He receives His Rod of Power,
the same Rod
used
since the foundation
of our planetary
Hierarchy,
And holds it forth to the Lord
of the World,
Who touches it

with His own mighty Rod,
causing a fresh
recharging
of its
electric capacity.
This ceremony takes place
at Shamballa.''
　　　Christ uses it
　　　at the time of the ceremony,
　　　first and second
　　　initiations,
　　　to sanctify the forces of personality
　　　so that they be used
　　　in service for humanity.
Christ uses
the Rod
also at the time
of Wesak Full Moon.
　　　Wesak Full Moon
　　　is the Full Moon
　　　of Taurus,
　　　at the time of which
　　　great alignment
　　　is established
　　　between Humanity, Hierarchy
　　　and
　　　Shamballa.
　　　　　This is the time
　　　　　when great Ones
　　　　　build a path
　　　　　of light and love
　　　　　and power
　　　　　between
　　　　　humanity
　　　　　and Shamballa.
The Rod of Sanat Kumara,

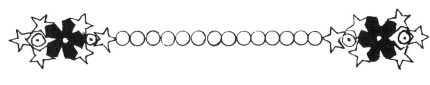

says the legend,
is hidden in "the East."
    "The Rod of the Lord
    of the World
    is charged afresh
    at each
    recurring world period,
    seven times
    in the history
    of a planetary
    scheme."
        This is the Mighty Rod
        which
        the Lord uses
      "To form a race,
      a nation,
      or a large
      organization,
      or
      when religious
      organizations and leaders
      need reawakening,
      or
      other organizations
      which
      are responsible
      for civilizations and culture
      or at the time
      of major
      initiations."
For example
the legend says
"At the third Initiation,
transfiguration,
the application
of the Rod

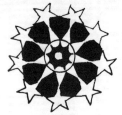
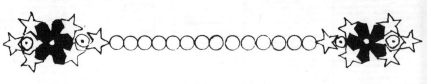

by the One Initiator,
the Sanat Kumara,
makes available
in a vastly more extensive manner,
the force of the higher Self...
and brings into play
on the physical
plane the entire energy
stored up
during numerous
incarnations
in the causal vehicle."
Legend says
there are other Rods,
the Rod of the Solar Logos,
which is hidden
in the "Heart of the Sun."
The Rod is called
the "Sevenfold Flaming Fire."
    "There is the Rod
     of Comic Logos,
     which is secreted
     in that central spot
     in the heavens
     around which
     our solar system revolves,
     and which
     is termed
     the central spiritual sun."
         Shamballa,
         Shamballa...

Many Teachings are given
to humanity
Through the Ashrams of the Hierarchy.
Teachings also are given
by Shamballa
To those Initiates who are entering
into the domain of inner fire.
The new-age Teaching
is
the Teaching of Fire,
electricity of the Spirit.
The disciples of Shamballa,
the Tower,
will carry the fire
into the seven departments
of human learning, and
experience.
This fire will create fusion
between them.
This fire will expand their horizons
and lead them into synthesis,
into universalism.
This fire will
reveal the ultimate goal
of each department
of learning.
The Teaching of fire
will be expressed
in politics,
revealing in the minds of leaders
the vision of
world unity
and divine will.

159

The Teaching of fire
will set aflame
the world educators
inspiring
all schools and universities
to the need
of transformation of human nature
and striving towards
self-actualization, beauty and enlightenment.
 The Teaching of fire
 will create
 a new orientation
 in philosophy,
 to reveal the meaning of life and space
 and to open the path
 to the will-to-evolve.
 The Teaching of Fire
 will create
 a new enthusiasm
 in the domain of art,
 the art will be the agent of **transfiguration** of
  human soul
 and will express
 the hidden beauty
 of the energy systems
 in the Cosmos.
The Teaching of Fire
will create
a new revelation in Science
and Science will occupy itself
with the unseen, subjective world,
with the fiery flowers of soul,
with the mysteries of life.
The Teaching of fire
will create
in religion a great shift

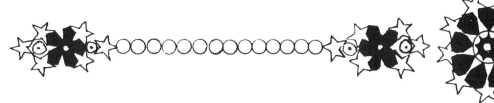

from crucifixion,
sin, mercy, punishment,
and hell,
to resurrection of spirit,
to communion with highest,
to joy and bliss.
    The Teaching of Fire
    will bring great harmony
    and synchronization
    in all departments of
    human endeavor.
    It will bring the spirit to share
    the deeper meaning of order,
    rhythm,
    and cooperation.
        The Teaching of fire
        will reveal
        the secrets of
        synthesis,
        and will use matter
        to express the beauties
        of the spirit.
        The Teaching of fire
        will unify all these endeavors
        into a greater symphony,
        in which the human spark
        will unfold and bloom.
        The Teaching of fire
        will reveal
        the art of contemplation,
        the art of inspiration,
        the art of contact,
        the art of sacrifice,
        the art of all-seeing eye,
        the art of conscious immortality.
            Men of fiery nature

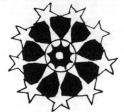
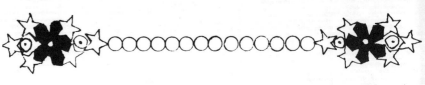

will study the Teaching of Fire
and transform
their lives
and turn into
living beauties,
living symphonies,
all giving,
all embracing.
The Teaching of Fire
will reveal
the fire in sound,
the fire in color,
the fire of the heart,
the fire of the spirit,
the fire of motion.
Man will realize
his nature
as fire
in the greater
greater Fire.
Man will solve his problems
.through the fire of spirit
through the fire of the heart...
  Shamballa!
  The Seat of Fire...

Shamballa,
Shamballa,
as I pronounce your name
I see flowers
blooming
on the sides of all roads of life;
I see
travellers on the path,
all dressed in rainbow colors,
and in rhythmic
dance
proceeding towards
a new Sunrise.
I see
the world
without hospitals,
without police,
without armies
and warships.
        I see human waves,
        in concentric
        circles, gathering
        around the Tower
        of Shamballa
        and all singing
        in a mighty chorus
            "Lord
            Your light led us
            from darkness to light,
            from the unreal to the Real,
            from death to Immortality,
            from chaos to Beauty.
            OM MANI PADME HUM
            OM. OM.

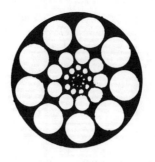

Shamballa,
Shamballa,
the open eye
into Cosmos.

OM.

My gratitude
to the great Master M.,
Djwhal Khul
Alice Bailey
H. P. Blavatsky
Nicholas Roerich
Helena Roerich
Great Lamas of the East
Great gratitude
from
the
bottom of my heart
for letting me know
about
this
fiery Legend
of
Shamballa.
OM.